A LITTLE TASTE OF
CAPE COD

a little taste of
CAPE COD

Recipes for Classic Dishes

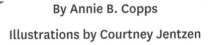

By Annie B. Copps

Illustrations by Courtney Jentzen

Bluestreak
BOOKS

Connected Dots Media would like to thank the team at Bluestreak Books for their generous work on this project, especially to publisher Chris Navratil for his smart, insightful creative inspiration.

Bluestreak Books is an imprint of Weldon Owen,
a Bonnier Publishing USA company
www.bonnierpublishingusa.com

Library of Congress-in-Publication Data is Available.
ISBN: 978-1-68188-350-2

First printed in 2018
10 9 8 7 6 5 4 3 2 1
2018 2019

Printed in China

Text and recipes by Annie B. Copps
Design by Margaux Keres
Illustrations by Courtney Jentzen

Produced exclusively for Bluestreak Books by Connected Dots Media,
www.connecteddotsmedia.com

CONTENTS

INTRODUCTION

Cape Cod is a very special spot, and for so many reasons. The diversity and sheer beauty of the land and sea have attracted many who call the Cape their year-round home. Others come just for the summer months, often continuing a passionate and dedicated annual tradition. Some stay for a long weekend or even just a day to enjoy a touch of the special flavors and feeling of the place, like eating a fried clam roll or sticking their feet in the sand. Whatever the reasons, once you cross the Bourne or Sagamore Bridge, you enter a new land, rich in beauty, history, and great eating.

This little book contains classic and traditional recipes showcasing a well-deserved respect for the geography and ecosystems of Cape Cod and the ingredients that emerge from them, as well as for the many populations and peoples who have lived here and influenced its culture for centuries. Also included are recipes with old-school roots but with a new twist to the ingredients or techniques.

Cape cooking has always been influenced by many factors. For starters, the geography and weather—some extreme, some nurturing—dictate what grows here and what season anything will appear. Each year we eagerly await corn, tomatoes, blueberries, and strawberries in the summer and turnips, cranberries, and apples in the fall, to name a few. Tradition and local culture dictate what we are taught to eat: so much of the cuisine is about the seashore, about being outside, and is often tuned to what can feed a crowd. It is also about what feeds our memories—one bite of lobster recalls one's very first bite of that sweet, briny, tender meat. Traditions in some villages of the Cape are still that of the first people, the Mashpee Wampanoag Native Americans; in other communities they come from early settlers like the Portuguese, Irish, Italian, Brazilian, and Jamaican. Enjoy this book in good health and good cheer.

COCKTAILS

Classic cocktails are experiencing a bit of a renaissance, and Cape Cod has not missed the boat.

For generations, Cape residents have been enjoying a fortifying beverage at festive occasions or just the end of a long summer (or winter) day. Adding local ingredients, like the blueberries and beach roses in this chapter, enhances longtime favorites and can provide inspiration for other interesting new twists. The key is to incorporate local flavors, whether in a nod (as with the cranberry and Clamato juices below) or freshly foraged (from the field or the farmers' market). Either way, the perfect balance of ingredients in these renditions creates classics and new classics alike.

Whether you make these cocktails by the pitcher or by the glass, have some fun with them by adding your own inspired garnishes or creative glassware.

All of the drinks in this chapter can be made for the 21-and-under set—just omit the alcohol and adjust with soda water.

3

CAPE CODDER

This cocktail, as popular almost everywhere in the country as it is in its namesake region, puts cranberry juice to good use and is as light and refreshing as it is beautiful and easy to make. You can easily morph this cocktail into its fancy city cousin, the Cosmopolitan, by making individual portions in a cocktail shaker filled with ice: Omit the soda, add a splash of triple sec, shake well, and strain into a chilled martini glass. This drink is also terrific made with white rum in place of the vodka.

SERVES 6

12 ounces vodka

12 ounces cranberry juice cocktail (sweetened cranberry juice)

¼ cup fresh lime juice

About 8 ounces club soda or sparkling water

Ice

6 fresh mint leaves, for garnish

1 In a large pitcher, combine the vodka, cranberry juice, and lime juice. Stir well to combine.

2 Add the club soda, stir to mix, and pour into 6 tall ice-filled glasses. Garnish each with a mint leaf and serve right away.

BLUEBERRY MOJITO

The cranberry may rule the berry kingdom on Cape Cod, but other berries, including blueberries, also thrive here towards the end of summer. Leave out the rum for a cooling nonalcoholic beverage on a hot day or at a beach picnic.

SERVES 6

1 pint blueberries, 18 reserved
for garnish

Leaves from 1 bunch fresh mint
(about 40 leaves), 6 reserved
for garnish

12 ounces club soda

12 ounces white rum

1/2 cup Simple Syrup
(recipe follows)

1/4 cup fresh lime juice

Ice

1 In a large pitcher, using a muddler or wooden spoon, muddle the blueberries and mint leaves with a splash of the soda, gently mashing to release the essential oils in the mint. Add the remaining soda, the rum, the Simple Syrup, and the lime juice. Stir well, then taste and adjust the flavors.

2 Pour into 6 tall ice-filled glasses. Garnish with the reserved blueberries and mint leaves and serve right away.

SIMPLE SYRUP

MAKES ABOUT 1/2 CUP

1/2 cup sugar

1/2 cup water

In a small saucepan over medium-high heat, combine the sugar and water and cook, stirring often, until the sugar has melted, about 5 minutes. Remove from the heat and let cool to room temperature. The syrup will keep in a tightly sealed jar in the refrigerator for up to 1 month.

BLOODY MARY WITH A COASTAL TWIST

This variation on the beloved weekend brunch libation is quite possibly the best addition out there to a slow and leisurely Sunday. A good Bloody Mary walks a fine line between cocktail and appetizer—and this one keeps its balance. The tomato-clam combo may raise a skeptic's eyebrows, but the delicate briny flavor only elevates this longtime favorite.

SERVES 6

12 ounces Clamato juice (or one part clam juice to two parts low-sodium tomato juice or V8)

8 ounces vodka

3 teaspoons Worcestershire sauce

2 teaspoons Tabasco sauce

1 teaspoon celery salt

1 teaspoon freshly ground black pepper

Juice of 2 limes

Ice

12 pitted green olives, for garnish

6 celery ribs, for garnish

1 In a pitcher, combine all of the ingredients except the ice, olives, and celery. Stir well to combine.

2 Pour into 6 tall ice-filled glasses. Garnish with the olives and celery ribs and serve right away.

SUMMER WIND

This special drink is summer in a glass—you just might hear Frank Sinatra's crooning voice in your head while you sip. Beach roses (*Rosa rugosa*) in various hues of pink and white grow wild all over Cape Cod. The petals are edible and can be used in a great range of recipes. If you are picking petals, be sure they are not on private property and that they have not been treated with chemicals.

SERVES 6

About 40 beach rose petals, brushed clean

12 ounces blueberry-flavored vodka (try Triple Eight from neighboring Nantucket)

10 ounces lemonade

Ice

½ pint blueberries, for garnish

About 20 fresh mint leaves, for garnish

1 In a large pitcher, using a muddler or wooden spoon, muddle the rose petals with a splash of the vodka, gently mashing to release the essential oils and subtle aroma in the petals. Add the remaining vodka and the lemonade. Stir well, then taste and adjust the flavors.

2 Pour into 6 tall ice-filled glasses. Garnish with the blueberries and mint leaves and serve right away.

APPETIZERS & SMALL BITES

Appetizers are meant to be small bites of flavorful food, eaten as a shared experience, served with a tipple of something to drink, and all enjoyed before sitting down to the table for the "real meal." In these days of exploring the joys of small plates, though, many a meal is made from an array of tapas, starters, or good old-fashioned hors d'oeuvres.

No matter what you call them or when or how you serve these appetizing bites, take advantage of what is in season and impeccably fresh. Maybe it's a full platter of Oysters with Mignonette Sauce (page 14) to be shared with lots of cocktail napkins and a pitcher of Cape Codders (page 4)—get the citronella candles going and gather around a table on the porch. Don't want to arrive empty-handed at the new neighbors' get-together? Smoked Bluefish Dip (page 19) or Classic Shrimp Cocktail (page 16) will please a crowd.

These simple seafood-centric delights are some of Neptune's finest creations for either starting off a wonderful meal or serving as a meal on their own. You decide.

9

GARLICKY MUSSELS WITH LINGUIÇA AND GRILLED BREAD

Mussels are a coastal favorite for all the right reasons: they are abundant, delicious, and usually moderately priced in comparison to other shellfish. The spicy *linguiça* sausage tossed in here is a nod to the delicious traditions of the Portuguese community of the Upper Cape and bumps up the overall flavor of the dish. Serve in individual bowls or arrange on a platter and serve in the center of a table to eat communally, using the bread to soak up the pan sauce.

SERVES 6

3 tablespoons extra-virgin olive oil

1½ tablespoons minced shallots

1 tablespoon minced garlic

¼ teaspoon red pepper flakes

1 cup dry white wine

6 ounces *linguiça* sausage, cut on the diagonal into slices about ¼ inch thick

2 pounds mussels, scrubbed and debearded

⅓ cup coarsely chopped fresh flat-leaf parsley

Grilled Bread for serving (recipe follows)

1 In a large saucepan or stock pot, heat the olive oil over medium heat. Add the shallots and cook, stirring, until softened and translucent, about 3 minutes. Add the garlic and red pepper flakes and cook until the garlic is fragrant, about 1 minute.

2 Add the wine and bring to a boil, stirring to scrape up any browned bits from the bottom of the pan. Cook until the liquid is reduced by half, 8 to 10 minutes. Stir in the *linguiça*, reduce the heat to maintain a gentle simmer, and cook, stirring occasionally, until the flavors are well developed, 10 to 15 minutes.

3 Add the mussels, cover the pan, and cook, stirring gently or shaking the pan occasionally, until the mussels open, about 10 minutes. Discard any mussels that did not open. Gently toss in about three-fourths of the parsley. Transfer the contents of the pan to a large serving bowl or deep platter or 6 individual bowls and garnish with the remaining parsley. Serve right away with the Grilled Bread.

GRILLED BREAD

MAKES 6 SLICES

6 thick (½-inch) slices crusty rustic bread or 12 thick (½-inch) slices baguette

Extra-virgin olive oil for brushing

2 cloves garlic, halved (optional)

Build a medium-hot fire in a charcoal or wood grill or preheat a gas grill, grill pan, or broiler to medium-high.

Lightly brush the bread slices on both sides with olive oil, then arrange on the grill rack or pan and grill, turning once, until nicely browned on both sides, about 3 minutes per side. Remove from the heat. When cool enough to handle, gently rub the bread with the cut sides of the garlic cloves, if using, until fragrant.

GRILLED CALAMARI

Referring to this dish by its Italian name *calamari* rather than "squid" may ease the nerves of the squeamish—but even the squid averse will want to try this tender-crisp grilled version, marinated and dressed with fragrant citrus, herbs, and spices.

SERVES 6

6 large squid (about 6 ounces each), bodies and tentacles separated and cleaned

1 tablespoon extra-virgin olive oil, plus more for the grill

1 tablespoon minced garlic

Zest and juice of 1 lemon

2 teaspoons ground cumin

½ teaspoon red pepper flakes

Kosher or sea salt

2 tablespoons chopped fresh cilantro or flat-leaf parsley

1 Lay the squid bodies flat on a cutting board with the open end facing you. Working with one squid at a time, slice up the length of one side to cut open the pocket. Lay the squid body flat. Lightly score the flesh, marking it vertically with the tip of a sharp knife without cutting all the way through— this will help keep the squid from curling up when cooking. Trim the tentacles and cut in half if they seem unmanageable for the fork or for biting.

2 In a shallow casserole dish or large bowl, whisk together the olive oil, garlic, lemon zest, cumin, red pepper flakes, and a pinch of salt. Add the squid bodies and tentacles and turn to coat well. Cover and let marinate in the refrigerator for at least 2 hours and up to 12 hours.

3 Remove the squid from the refrigerator 30 minutes before grilling to take the chill off. Build a medium-hot fire in a charcoal or wood grill or preheat a gas grill or grill pan to medium-high. Oil the grill rack or pan well.

4 Remove the squid from the marinade; shake off and discard any excess. Lay the squid bodies and tentacles on the grill rack and cook, undisturbed, for about 2 minutes. Turn and grill on the second side for about 2 minutes longer; the squid should be nicely grill marked on both sides and charred on the edges and the flesh should be opaque throughout.

5 Arrange the grilled squid on a platter or individual serving plates. Sprinkle with salt, the lemon juice, and the cilantro. Serve right away.

OYSTERS WITH MIGNONETTE SAUCE

Oysters are all about their provenance. On the East Coast, just about all the oysters growing are from the same species, *Crassostrea virginica*, but their breeding ground, shape, and size define how they taste. The flavor changes depending on additional factors like what else is growing alongside the oysters, the tides and currents, and the salinity of the water. The waters off Cape Cod produce fantastic oysters—especially (and famously) the ones from the villages of Cotuit and Wellfleet.

Every lover of fresh raw oysters has their preferences for how to eat them. This classic mignonette sauce enhances the briny, fresh-from-the-sea flavor of the oysters without overpowering their delicate personality.

Shucking oysters can be a challenge; be sure to wear heavy gloves and use a sturdy oyster knife, and seek out instructions if needed. If you're unsure, you can always have your fishmonger open them for you for a few cents more each.

SERVES 2 OR 3

¼ cup champagne or red wine vinegar

1 tablespoon minced shallots

¼ teaspoon freshly ground black pepper

12 medium (3- to 4-inch) oysters, freshly shucked, muscles loosened from the bottom shells

1 In a small bowl, stir together the vinegar, shallots, and pepper. Set aside.

2 Arrange the oysters in their half shells in a large bowl or platter on a bed of ice.

3 Spoon some of the mignonette sauce on top of each oyster. Serve chilled.

CLASSIC SHRIMP COCKTAIL

People always go crazy for shrimp, no matter how they're prepared. This simple, classic appetizer never goes out of style, because it is just so darn good.

SERVES 4

1 yellow onion, sliced

½ lemon, sliced

2 sprigs fresh thyme

2 bay leaves, torn in half

1 tablespoon whole black peppercorns

About 2 quarts cold water

1 pound shell-on, deveined jumbo shrimp

Cocktail Sauce for serving (recipe follows), chilled

1 In a large stock pot, combine the onion, the lemon slices and a squeeze of their juice, the thyme, bay leaves, peppercorns, and cold water. Bring to a simmer and cook for 15 to 20 minutes to allow the flavors to infuse the water.

2 Place a large bowl of ice and water next to the stovetop. Raise the heat to maintain a low boil in the pot and add the shrimp. Cook until they are bright pink, curled up, and no longer translucent in the center, about 5 minutes. Using a slotted spoon, immediately transfer the shrimp to the bowl of ice water and immerse to stop the cooking. When cooled, drain and pat dry. Peel and discard the shells.

3 Arrange the shrimp on a serving platter and serve with the chilled Cocktail Sauce. For individual servings, spoon 1 tablespoon of the Cocktail Sauce into the center of a martini glass and hang 6 or more shrimp around the rim of the glass. Serve right away.

COCKTAIL SAUCE

MAKES ABOUT ½ CUP

½ cup ketchup

1 tablespoon prepared horseradish

1 teaspoon fresh lemon juice

¼ teaspoon Worcestershire sauce

3 drops Tabasco sauce (or your favorite hot-pepper sauce), or to taste

In a small bowl, stir together the ketchup, horseradish, lemon juice, Worcestershire sauce, and Tabasco until well combined. Refrigerate until chilled, at least 15 minutes.

SMOKED BLUEFISH DIP

Bluefish has a strong flavor and oily texture that puts many people off. Fear not: smoking the fillets mellows the flavor, and mixing in a few fresh and bright ingredients turns this ugly duckling into a true swan. This is a great dip to have in the fridge ready to go, as it always gets gobbled up. Double the recipe and freeze it in small batches so you always have some in a pinch.

MAKES ABOUT 2 CUPS; SERVES 4

8 ounces mascarpone cheese or cream cheese, at room temperature

3 scallions, white and tender green parts, finely chopped

2 tablespoons finely chopped fresh dill, plus small sprigs for garnish

1 tablespoon Worcestershire sauce

1 tablespoon fresh lemon juice

4 to 6 dashes of Tabasco or other hot-pepper sauce

8 ounces skinless, boneless smoked bluefish, flaked into chunks

Thinly sliced rye, pumpernickel, or black bread, toasted and lightly buttered, for serving

3 or 4 radishes, trimmed and thinly sliced, for serving

1 In a bowl, combine the mascarpone with the scallions, chopped dill, Worcestershire sauce, lemon juice, and Tabasco and stir to mix well. Gently fold the bluefish into the mascarpone mixture until evenly distributed.

2 Scoop the dip into a serving bowl and garnish with the dill sprigs. Serve with the toasted bread and radishes.

SOFT-SHELL CLAMS STEAMED IN BEER WITH DRAWN BUTTER

Cover the table with newspaper, place a large bowl for discarded shells in the center, and go to town with this slightly messy but very traditional—and very fun—appetizer. To eat steamers, use your fingers to strip away and discard the tough skin covering the siphon of the clam (that muscular tube sticking out of the shell). Rinse the siphon in the reserved hot cooking broth to wash away any remaining grit or sand, then use it as a handle to dip the clam in the melted butter, and enjoy.

SERVES 4 TO 6

2 cups cornmeal

1 tablespoon kosher salt

3 to 4 pounds soft-shell steamer clams (see Note)

Two 12-ounce bottles of your favorite IPA beer

Drawn Butter for serving (recipe follows), warmed

1 In a large stock pot, combine the cornmeal, salt, clams, and enough water to cover the clams by about 3 inches. Let rest for at least 3 hours or up to overnight in the refrigerator or other very cool place. This will help rid the steamers of any sand or grit.

2 Drain the clams and discard the cornmeal soaking water. Rinse and scrub the clams thoroughly. Rinse out the pot and pour in the beer. Add the clams and cover the pot. Bring to a boil over high heat, then reduce the heat to maintain a bare simmer and steam the clams until the shells are wide open, 5 to 10 minutes. Remove the pot from the heat and discard any clams that did not open.

3 Using a slotted spoon, transfer the cooked clams to a serving bowl. Strain the cooking liquid through a sieve lined with cheesecloth into a bowl and place the hot broth on the table for diners to give the clams another rinse before eating them (see recipe introduction). Serve right away with the Drawn Butter for dipping.

NOTE: Soft-shell clams, or steamers, do not have "soft" shells, but rather they have thin, brittle shells that easily break. They picked up the nickname "steamers" because their shells are easy to open and their long siphon, or neck, is easy to pluck out of the shell and dip into drawn butter, making them ideal for steaming and dipping.

DRAWN BUTTER

MAKES ABOUT 1¾ CUPS
1 pound unsalted butter

In a small saucepan over medium heat, melt the butter. Bring to a gentle simmer and cook until the cloudy, white milk solids separate and sink to the bottom of the pan. Remove from the heat and let rest for 5 minutes. Pour off the clear, golden yellow liquid into a clean small saucepan and keep warm until ready to serve. Discard the white milky liquid.

STUFFED QUAHOGS

Buttery Ritz crackers are traditional in this filling and add a rich crunch that is hard to beat, but feel free to substitute panko bread crumbs or other crackers crumbs, if you prefer. To keep the clams upright while baking, place each on a nest of salt.

SERVES 2 TO 4

12 large Quahog clams, scrubbed and rinsed

4 tablespoons unsalted butter, plus 1 tablespoon, melted

½ cup finely chopped yellow onion

½ cup finely chopped celery

¼ cup seeded and finely chopped green or red bell pepper

2 tablespoons chopped fresh flat-leaf parsley

1 tablespoon freshly grated Parmesan cheese

¼ teaspoon freshly ground black pepper

¼ teaspoon Worcestershire sauce

12 Ritz crackers, finely crushed (about ½ cup)

1 cup kosher salt or sea salt

Paprika for garnish

1 Put the clams in a large stock pot and add enough water to cover by about 2 inches. Bring to a boil over high heat, then reduce the heat to maintain a simmer. Cover and cook until the clams are wide open, 6 to 10 minutes. Remove the clams from the pot and let cool. Discard any clams that did not open.

2 When cool enough to handle, remove the clam meat, transfer to a cutting board, and mince finely. Set aside on a plate. (If not serving within an hour, cover and refrigerate.) Break apart the clamshells at their hinges; rinse and dry. Choose 12 of the cleanest, best-looking shells and set aside. Discard the remaining shells. Preheat the oven to 350°F.

3 In a sauté pan over medium heat, melt
the 4 tablespoons butter. Add the onion,
celery, and bell pepper and cook, stirring
gently, until softened and fragrant, about
5 minutes. Remove from the heat and
stir in the parsley, cheese, pepper, and
Worcestershire sauce. Add ¼ cup of the
cracker crumbs and mix well. Pour off
any clam liquid that accumulated on the
plate and reserve. Add the minced clams
to the vegetable mixture. If it seems dry, add
the reserved clam liquid as needed. Divide the filling
among the 12 shells and pack firmly. In a small bowl,
stir together the remaining cracker crumbs and the
melted butter and sprinkle over the filling.

4 In another small bowl, combine the salt and, working in a
teaspoon or two at a time, add just enough water to create a
sandy paste. On a rimmed baking sheet, make 12 salt "nests" and
place each clam on top of a nest. Bake until the crumbs on top are
crunchy and deep brown in color, 10 to 15 minutes. Sprinkle with
paprika and serve hot.

SOUPS, SANDWICHES & SIDES

The native ingredients of Cape Cod were crucial to the survival of the first people of this land, the Mashpee Wampanoag tribe. They foraged and cultivated the land and sea, and honored the bounty. They showed the European settlers what they knew about cranberries, beach plums, sea beans, and, of course, all the wonderful seafood. The Europeans survived their first years because of this and soon used this information to craft new foods, forged from their old ways. With each new person who settles on this beautiful land comes new ideas on what to do with local ingredients and traditions.

Here, time-tested favorites such as lobster bisque and the indulgent lobster roll are left alone in their perfection, local turnips are turned into a luxurious mash, sweet corn is transformed into a rich and hearty pudding, and Provincetown takes the lead with a soul-satisfying soup.

25

LOBSTER BISQUE

This is a rich and silky-smooth bisque, teeming with concentrated lobster flavor. The prices of these prized crustaceans go up and down; if they are up, save this dish for a birthday, anniversary, or other special occasion. If lobster prices are down, make it anytime—even a Monday-night dinner. The splash of sherry vinegar at the end is not traditional, but it gently elevates all of the flavors and brightens the lushness.

If you are uncomfortable cutting up live lobsters, have your fishmonger do it for you, but be sure you are ready to use the lobster pieces straight away.

SERVES 6

¼ cup vegetable oil

Two 1½-pound live lobsters, split in half lengthwise (body and tail), claws separated

1 yellow onion, finely chopped

2 sprigs fresh thyme

2 tablespoons tomato paste

½ cup brandy

2 quarts heavy cream

1½ teaspoons sherry vinegar

1 Heat the oil in a large, heavy-bottomed saucepan over medium heat. Add the lobster pieces, onion, and thyme sprigs and sauté until the lobster shells turn red and the meat is opaque throughout, about 8 minutes.

2 Add the tomato paste and cook, stirring often, until slightly browned, about 3 minutes. Remove the pan from the heat and add the brandy. Using a long match, carefully ignite the brandy to cook off the alcohol. After the flames have subsided, return the pan to medium heat and cook, stirring, until the liquid is reduced to about 1 tablespoon, 3 to 5 minutes. Stir in the cream and bring to a boil. Reduce the heat to maintain a gentle simmer and cook until the bisque is thickened and the flavors have fully developed, 30 to 40 minutes.

3 Remove the pan from the heat. Using tongs, transfer the lobster pieces to a plate and let cool slightly. When cool enough to handle, remove the meat from the tail, claw, and knuckle shells; discard the shells and bodies. Chop the larger pieces of meat into 1-inch pieces and return all of the meat to the pan. Stir in the sherry vinegar. Rewarm gently over low heat, if needed.

4 Ladle into 6 individual bowls, dividing the lobster meat evenly, and serve hot.

NEW ENGLAND CLAM CHOWDER

Like tomato sauce in Italy, for every home on the Cape, there is a slightly different way to make clam chowder—and they are all "the best." Some are thick and potato heavy, others less viscous and more herbaceous. This one is right in the middle.

SERVES 6

7 pounds cherrystone clams, scrubbed and rinsed

4 strips bacon, finely chopped

1 yellow onion, finely diced

1 celery rib, finely diced

2 tablespoons all-purpose flour

3 large red potatoes, peeled and cut into ½-inch dice

3 sprigs fresh thyme

1 bay leaf, broken in half

1 cup heavy cream

2 tablespoons chopped fresh flat-leaf parsley

1 Put the clams in a large soup or stock pot, add 3 cups water, and place over medium-high heat. Cover and bring to a simmer. Cook, shaking the pot occasionally, just until the clams open, about 10 minutes. Using a slotted spoon, transfer the cooked clams to a bowl and set aside. Discard any clams that did not open. Strain the cooking liquid into a bowl through a sieve lined with cheesecloth or a coffee filter and set aside.

2 Rinse and dry the pot thoroughly and place over medium heat. Add the bacon and cook until browned but not crispy and most of the fat has been rendered, about 10 minutes. Using the slotted spoon, transfer to a paper towel–lined plate to drain.

continued

3 Add the onion and celery to the pot with the bacon fat
   and cook, stirring often, until the onion is softened and
fragrant, about 10 minutes. Whisk in the flour and cook until
lightly browned. Add the reserved clam broth 1 cup at a
time, whisking vigorously to remove any lumps of flour.
Add the potatoes, thyme sprigs, and bay leaf and simmer
for 10 minutes.

4 Remove the clams from their shells, reserving any liquid that
   accumulated in the bowl, and chop the meat coarsely. Discard
the shells. Add the clams and any liquid in the bowl to the pot
along with the cream. Cook, stirring gently once or twice,
just until the potatoes are tender and the clams are heated
through, 3 to 4 minutes longer. Remove and discard the thyme
sprigs and bay leaf. Stir in the parsley.

5 Ladle into 6 individual bowls, dividing the clam meat evenly,
   and serve hot.

PORTUGUESE KALE AND SAUSAGE SOUP

Every culture has their own chicken soup, so to speak—liquid gold that is satisfying on any day and in tougher times can lessen the pain of everything from the common cold to a broken heart. In Provincetown, at the very tip of the Cape, there is a thriving Portuguese community, and this is their panacea: *caldo verde*. Make a double batch for the good times and the bad.

SERVES 6

1 tablespoon extra-virgin olive oil

1 yellow onion, chopped

1 pound *linguiça* sausage, cut into slices about ¼ inch thick

2 tablespoons minced garlic

4 cups homemade or low-sodium chicken stock

1 pound kale, tough stems and spines removed, coarsely chopped

2 large potatoes, russet or your preference, peeled and cut into ½-inch cubes

1½ cups cooked cannellini beans

Kosher salt or sea salt and freshly ground black pepper

1 In a large soup pot, heat the olive oil over medium heat. Add the onion and *linguiça* and cook, stirring often, until the onion is softened and translucent, about 8 minutes. Stir in the garlic and cook until fragrant, about 1 minute longer.

2 Add the chicken stock and kale and bring to a simmer. Cover and cook gently, stirring occasionally, for 20 minutes. Add the potatoes, re-cover, and simmer until tender, for 20 minutes. Add the beans and cook for a minute or two to heat through. Adjust the consistency with a little water, if you like. Season with salt and pepper to taste.

3 Ladle into 6 individual bowls and serve hot.

FRIED CLAM ROLL

It's hard to beat this seaside classic: warm, crispy nuggets of sweet clam, bursting with briny flavor in each bite, all swaddled in a soft, crunchy, buttery toasted bun. These are best eaten while wearing a damp swimsuit and a touch of sunburn.

MAKES 6 SANDWICHES

2 cups all-purpose flour

1 cup fine-ground cornmeal

1 teaspoon kosher salt or sea salt, plus more for sprinkling

1 teaspoon freshly ground black pepper

1 pound freshly shucked clams, drained

Vegetable oil for frying (about 3 cups)

2 tablespoons unsalted butter, at room temperature

6 hot-dog buns

6 large butter (Bibb) lettuce leaves

Tartar Sauce for serving (recipe follows)

1 In a large bowl, whisk together the flour, cornmeal, salt, and pepper.

2 Add about 1 cup of the clams to the flour mixture. Stir gently to thoroughly coat the clams in the mixture. Transfer the coated clams to a large plate or shallow bowl. Repeat with the remaining clams.

3 Pour oil into a large saucepan or deep fryer to a depth of about 3 inches and heat to 375°F on a deep-frying thermometer. Place a rimmed baking sheet lined with paper towels nearby.

4 Using a slotted spoon or skimmer, carefully add about half of the clams to the hot oil (do not crowd the pan or the oil temperature will drop too low and the clams will get soggy) and fry until crispy and golden brown, about 2 minutes. Using the spoon or skimmer, transfer the fried clams to the prepared baking sheet to drain. Sprinkle with salt while still warm. Repeat to fry, drain, and salt the remaining clams.

5 Spread the butter on both sides of the hot-dog buns. In a large sauté pan over medium heat, toast the buns, turning once, until deeply browned on both sides, about 2 minutes per side. Lay a lettuce leaf inside each bun and divide the fried clams evenly among them. Drizzle with the Tartar Sauce or serve it on the side. Serve warm.

TARTAR SAUCE

MAKES ABOUT 1 CUP

1 cup mayonnaise

2 tablespoons sweet pickle relish or finely chopped pickles

1 teaspoon fresh lemon juice

¼ teaspoon Tabasco sauce

In a bowl, combine the mayonnaise, pickle relish, lemon juice, and Tabasco and stir to mix well. Refrigerate until ready to serve.

LOBSTER ROLL

There are many ways to make a lobster roll. This one is straightforward, with no mucking about—the point is to be able to taste the lobster, the distinct sweet flavor of which is also subtle and shouldn't get lost among stronger flavors or too much mayonnaise.

It is important to use New England–style hot-dog buns. These soft, straight-sided, flat-bottomed rolls are ideal for buttering and toasting on both sides, which lends a lot of flavor and texture to the lobster roll.

MAKES 6 SANDWICHES

2 pounds cooked lobster meat, coarsely chopped

3 tablespoons chopped fresh flat-leaf parsley

3 tablespoons coarsely chopped fresh celery leaves

About ¾ cup mayonnaise

2 tablespoons unsalted butter, at room temperature

6 New England–style hot-dog buns

6 large butter (Bibb) lettuce leaves

1 In a bowl, combine the lobster meat, parsley, and celery leaves. Add half of the mayonnaise, fold gently to combine, and taste. The lobster should be the predominant flavor, but there should be (just) enough mayonnaise to hold the ingredients together; add more mayonnaise if necessary.

2 Spread the butter on both sides of the hot-dog buns. In a large sauté pan over medium heat, toast the buns, turning once, until deeply browned on both sides, about 2 minutes per side. Lay a lettuce leaf inside each bun and divide the lobster mixture evenly among them. Serve right away.

CORN PUDDING

This Cape Cod signature pudding is a must when corn is in season, but frozen and defrosted corn works fine when you're craving it other times of year.

This recipe is delicious in its as-is simplicity, but you can also mix it up with infinite variations like adding sautéed zucchini, leeks, wild mushrooms, and/or crisp-cooked crumbled bacon.

SERVES 8

Unsalted butter for greasing, plus 2 tablespoons

2 tablespoons chopped scallions, white and tender green parts

3 cups fresh corn kernels

3 sprigs fresh thyme

1 teaspoon kosher salt

½ teaspoon white pepper

3 large whole eggs plus 3 large egg yolks

3 cups heavy cream

⅓ cup all-purpose flour

⅓ cup fine-ground cornmeal

1 tablespoon chopped fresh flat-leaf parsley

1 Preheat the oven to 325°F. Generously butter a 2-quart baking dish.

2 In a large sauté pan over medium-high heat, melt 1 tablespoon of the butter. Add the scallions, corn, and thyme sprigs, stir well, and cook, undisturbed, until the corn is lightly browned and the thyme is fragrant, 2 to 3 minutes. Remove from the heat and discard the thyme sprigs. Stir in the salt and white pepper and set aside.

3 In a large bowl, combine the whole eggs and egg yolks with the cream and whisk until thoroughly blended. Whisk in the flour, cornmeal, and parsley. Add the corn mixture from the sauté pan and stir to mix well. Pour into the prepared baking dish and bake until lightly browned on top and the pudding is set in the middle, 30 to 40 minutes. Let rest for about 5 minutes, then serve warm.

EASTHAM TURNIP MASH

Located on the Lower Cape, the village of Eastham is known for its marvelous turnips. Each November there is a cooking contest, and every year the recipes get better and better. With a mild sweetness and earthy notes, Eastham turnips are indeed special and different from other turnips. Whether it's due to the soil or the fresh salt air or some other factor, the magic in these turnips makes for a treat to eat.

Try this comforting mash that uses equal parts potato, or simply cut the turnips into strips, toss with olive oil and salt, and roast until deeply browned.

SERVES 6

1 pound turnips (about 2 large), peeled and cut into 4-inch pieces

1 pound russet or Yukon Gold potatoes (about 4 medium), peeled and cut into 4-inch pieces

4 cups whole milk

1 teaspoon kosher salt or sea salt

½ teaspoon white pepper

½ teaspoon freshly grated nutmeg

1 bay leaf, broken in half

1 tablespoon unsalted butter

1 In a large saucepan over medium-high heat, combine the turnips, potatoes, milk, salt, white pepper, nutmeg, and bay leaf and bring to a gentle boil. Cook until the turnips and potatoes are very tender and most of the milk has been absorbed, about 20 minutes. Remove from the heat.

2 Discard the bay leaf and add the butter. Using a potato masher or large fork or spoon, mash the mixture until mostly smooth. Taste and adjust the seasoning. Serve warm.

MAIN COURSES

Whether served in the dining room on your finest china with starched linens and polished silverware or outside on a picnic table with paper plates, these main dishes are meant to be shared with family and friends in any setting.

This chapter includes Cape Cod classics such as broiled fish and mussels with spaghetti, as well as international gems such as jerk chicken and *feijoada* that represent the diverse community that makes up the Cape. All of these dishes are relatively easy to prepare, but note, some need to be started a day in advance to really make an impact.

BABY BACK RIBS WITH CRANBERRY BARBECUE SAUCE

The Northeast may not be the first place one thinks of for great barbecue, but you are likely to reconsider that thought after trying these ribs. This recipe puts a Cape Cod twist on traditional barbecue with the addition of cranberries in the sauce. The tartness of the berries with the sweet, sour, and spicy notes of the sauce is a revelation.

SERVES 6

1 tablespoon ground cumin

1 tablespoon ground coriander

2 teaspoons kosher salt or sea salt

1 teaspoon freshly ground black pepper

2 racks baby back ribs (about 2 pounds each)

¼ cup canola or vegetable oil

3 cups fresh or thawed frozen cranberries

One 12-ounce can thawed frozen orange juice concentrate

¼ cup honey

3 tablespoons cider vinegar

1 tablespoon Sriracha or your favorite hot-pepper sauce

1 Build a medium-hot fire in a charcoal or wood grill or preheat a gas grill or grill pan to medium-high.

2 In a small bowl, whisk together the cumin, coriander, salt, and pepper. Rub the rib racks all over with the oil. Rub the spice mixture on both sides of the ribs. Grill the ribs, uncovered, for about 5 minutes per side. Transfer the ribs to two large baking dishes; set aside.

3 Preheat the oven to 300°F. In a saucepan over high heat, combine cranberries, orange juice concentrate, honey, cider vinegar, and Sriracha and cook, stirring often, until reduced by half, about 10 minutes. (The sauce can be made up to 4 days in advance and kept, tightly covered, in the refrigerator.) Reserve 1 cup of the sauce and pour the rest over the ribs, dividing it evenly between the dishes. Turn each rack a few times to coat the ribs well.

4 Cover the dishes with aluminum foil, place in the oven, and bake until the meat has begun to shrink away from the bones, the tips of the bones are exposed, and the meat is tender, 1½ to 2 hours. Remove from the oven and let rest for 5 to 10 minutes. Meanwhile, gently reheat the reserved 1 cup barbecue sauce.

5 To serve, slice the ribs between the bones and arrange on plates. Drizzle the warmed sauce over the ribs or serve alongside as a dipping sauce.

PORK VINHA D'ALHOS

Another Portuguese favorite, this dish hails from the semitropical island of Madeira. The preparation of pork slowly marinated in garlic and wine is typically served during the Christmas holidays, but really, these chops work well on any night. The key is marinating the pork for at least 12 hours and serving it with crusty bread cooked in the pan juices.

SERVES 6

1 cup red wine vinegar

1 cup dry white wine

10 cloves garlic, chopped

3 bay leaves, broken in half

1 tablespoon freshly ground black pepper

2 teaspoons red pepper flakes (Portuguese *piri-piri* or malagueta, if you can find them)

1 teaspoon paprika

½ cup olive oil

Six 6- to 8-ounce pork chops

Kosher salt or sea salt

6 slices rustic crusty bread

2 tablespoons chopped fresh flat-leaf parsley

1 In a large bowl or plastic storage bin, combine the vinegar, wine, garlic, bay leaves, black pepper, red pepper flakes, paprika, and ¼ cup of the olive oil. Add the pork chops and turn to coat well. Cover and let marinate in the refrigerator for at least 12 hours and up to 3 days.

2 Remove the meat from the marinade, shaking off the excess. Pat dry with paper towels and season with salt on all sides.

3 In a large sauté pan, heat the remaining ¼ cup olive oil over high heat. Add the pork chops and cook, turning once, until well browned on both sides, about 3 minutes per side. Transfer to individual plates. Add the bread slices to the hot oil remaining in the pan and fry until nicely browned on both sides, about 2 minutes per side. Divide the bread among the plates, garnish the chops and bread with the parsley, and serve right away.

BROILED COD WITH BREAD CRUMBS AND LEMON BUTTER

Simple, easy, traditional, and delicious. What more could you ask for? But here's a bonus: You don't have to wait for cod to come into season—you can make this recipe with any of your favorite firm white fish.

SERVES 6

5 tablespoons unsalted butter, at room temperature

¾ cup unseasoned panko bread crumbs

2 teaspoons chopped fresh thyme

1 tablespoon minced shallots

1 tablespoon grated lemon zest

1 tablespoon fresh lemon juice

Six 6-ounce cod fillets

1 Position a rack 6 inches from the heat source and preheat the broiler. In a large sauté pan over medium-high heat, melt 2 tablespoons of the butter. Add the bread crumbs and thyme and stir well to coat the bread crumbs. Remove from the heat and set aside.

2 In a small bowl, combine the remaining 3 tablespoons butter, the shallots, and lemon zest and juice. Lay the fillets on a rimmed baking sheet. Spread the lemon butter in an even layer on top of each of the fillets, dividing it evenly. Distribute the bread crumbs over the butter and press gently to help them adhere.

3 Broil the fish until just cooked through and the bread crumbs are nicely browned, about 5 minutes. (If the bread crumbs brown too quickly and the fish is not cooked through, adjust the distance of the baking sheet from the broiler.) Serve right away.

FEIJOADA

Like their Portuguese cousins in Provincetown, for many generations a strong group of Brazilians have established communities throughout the Cape. This is their national dish.

There are loads of variations on the master meat-and-bean medley of *feijoada*; this one is gussied up with pork chops. Often *feijoada* is made with trotters and tails—feel free to add them here, if you like.

SERVES 8

2 pounds dried black beans

2 pounds pork chops or ribs

½ pound slab bacon, cut into slices about ¼ inch thick

1 pound smoked pork sausage, cut into slices about ¼ inch thick

About 2 tablespoons vegetable oil

2 yellow onions, chopped

3 tablespoons minced garlic

Pinch of red pepper flakes

2 bay leaves, broken in half

1 tablespoon white wine or cider vinegar

Kosher salt or sea salt and freshly ground black pepper

Steamed white rice for serving

2 oranges, thinly sliced, for garnish

1 In a large soup or stock pot, combine the beans, pork chops, and bacon. Add water to cover by about 1 inch and bring to a boil over high heat. Reduce the heat to medium-low, cover, and simmer gently, stirring occasionally, until the beans and meat are almost tender, 2 to 2½ hours. Skim off and discard any foam that accumulates on top and add water as needed to keep the beans covered while the *feijoada* cooks.

2 Add the sausage and cook until the beans are very tender, the pork chops are falling-apart tender, and the broth is very flavorful, about 30 minutes longer.

3 In a large sauté pan or over medium heat, add enough oil to coat the bottom of the pan. Add the onions and cook, stirring often, until softened and fragrant, about 8 minutes. Add the garlic, red pepper flakes, and bay leaves and cook until the garlic is fragrant, about 1 minute. Add the bean mixture and stir well. Bring to a simmer. Remove and discard the bay leaves. Stir in the vinegar. Season to taste with salt and black pepper.

4 Serve over the rice, garnished with the oranges slices.

JAMAICAN JERK CHICKEN WITH RICE AND BEANS

Cape Cod celebrates its strong Jamaican community, and the population embraces the rich culture of the warm Caribbean islands as a whole—especially the food and music. Jerk chicken is a spicy dish, so use your judgment when adding heat and adjust to your taste. The longer the chicken marinates, the more flavorful (aka spicy) this will be. (If handling raw Scotch bonnet peppers, use kitchen gloves and wash your hands and the gloves well.) Rice and beans—or as the combo is often called in the Caribbean, "rice and peas"—are a must to serve alongside.

SERVES 10

2 cups chopped scallions, white and tender green parts

1 small yellow onion, coarsely chopped

2 Scotch bonnet chiles or 4 to 6 habanero or jalapeño chiles, stems removed

One 2-inch piece fresh ginger, peeled and coarsely chopped

6 cloves garlic, smashed

2 tablespoons dark brown sugar

2 tablespoons ground allspice

1 teaspoon ground cardamom

½ teaspoon freshly grated nutmeg

½ cup vegetable oil

2 tablespoons dark rum

1 tablespoon soy sauce

1 tablespoon apple cider vinegar

Zest and juice of 2 limes

Kosher salt or sea salt

Two 3½-pound chickens, quartered (2 breasts, 2 legs, and 2 thighs each)

Rice and Beans for serving (recipe follows)

continued

1 In a blender or food processor, combine the scallions, onion, chiles, ginger, garlic, brown sugar, allspice, cardamom, nutmeg, oil, rum, soy sauce, and vinegar and process to a purée. Stir in the lime zest and juice and season with salt to taste.

2 Gently pat the chicken pieces dry with paper towels and place in a large casserole or plastic storage container. Pour the marinade all over the chicken and turn to coat thoroughly. Cover and let marinate in the refrigerator for at least 12 hours and up to 48 hours, turning once or twice during the marinating time.

3 Build a medium-hot fire in a charcoal or wood grill or preheat a gas grill to medium-low.

4 Remove the chicken pieces from the marinade and shake off the excess. Arrange the chicken on the grill rack over the medium-low heat in the gas grill or over indirect heat in the charcoal grill. Close the lid and let cook undisturbed for about 30 minutes. The chicken should be golden brown but not cooked all the way through.

5 Turn the chicken pieces, raise the heat to medium-high in the gas grill or move to a hotter area of the grill in the charcoal grill, close the lid, and cook for 10 minutes longer. The thighs should be cooked through at this point; remove from the heat and set aside.

6 Turn the remaining chicken pieces, close the lid, and continue cooking until the internal temperature reaches 155°F on an instant-read thermometer when inserted into a thick part of the breast but away from the bone. The skin should be dark brown and chicken juices should run clear when the meat is cut into. For larger pieces, this can take up to 1 hour total.

7 Serve hot with the Rice and Beans.

RICE AND BEANS

SERVES 10

¼ cup canola or vegetable oil

½ cup minced yellow onion

1 tablespoon minced garlic

2 teaspoons minced jalapeño chile

2 cups long-grain white rice

1¾ cups coconut milk

2½ cups homemade or low-sodium chicken stock

One 15-ounce can red kidney beans, rinsed and drained

1 sprig fresh thyme

2 bay leaves, broken in half

Kosher salt and freshly ground black pepper

In a saucepan, heat the oil over medium-high heat. Add the onions and cook, stirring often, until softened and fragrant, about 8 minutes. Add the garlic and jalapeño and cook until the garlic is fragrant, about 1 minute.

Add the rice and stir so that all the grains are well coated with the oil and vegetables. Do not let the rice brown. Stir in the coconut milk, chicken stock, beans, thyme sprig, and bay leaves. Bring to a boil, then reduce the heat to the lowest setting, cover, and cook, undisturbed, until the rice is fully cooked, about 20 minutes. Remove the pan from the heat and set aside, covered, for 10 minutes. Remove and discard the thyme sprig and bay leaves. Fluff the rice with a fork. Season with salt and pepper to taste. Serve warm.

MUSSELS WITH SPAGHETTI & RED SAUCE

A stalwart of Southern Italian cooks came to these shores generations ago with the many Italians who made Cape Cod their new home. They brought with them an incredible method for cooking these rock-dwelling shellfish with sweet, tender flesh. The pristine mussels found in both the bay- and ocean-side waters of the Cape are well suited for this dish.

SERVES 6

2 tablespoons olive oil

1 large yellow onion, finely chopped (about 1½ cups)

1 tablespoon minced garlic

¼ teaspoon red pepper flakes

½ cup dry red wine

One 14½-ounce can tomato purée, preferably San Marzano

3 sprigs fresh thyme

2 pounds mussels, scrubbed and debearded

Kosher salt

1 pound spaghetti or other strand pasta

¼ cup chopped fresh flat-leaf parsley

1 Bring a large pot of water to a low simmer over medium heat and cover. In a saucepan, heat the olive oil over medium-high heat. Add the onion and cook until softened and fragrant, about 8 minutes. Add the garlic and red pepper flakes and cook until the garlic is fragrant, about 1 minute.

2 Stir in the wine and cook until there is about 1 tablespoon of liquid left in the pan, about 5 minutes. Stir in the tomato purée and thyme sprigs and cook for 5 minutes. Bring to a simmer and add the mussels. Cover the pan and cook, gently shaking the pan occasionally, until the mussels open, 2 to 4 minutes. Discard any mussels that do not open.

3 Using tongs, transfer the mussels to a bowl and let sit until cool enough
   to handle; leave the sauce in the pan over very low heat. Leaving the meat
and whole mussels in the bowl, remove half of the mussels from their shells
(discard the shells) and leave half in their shells. Cover the bowl and set aside.

4 Raise the heat under the water, add a generous amount of salt, and bring to
   a boil. Add the spaghetti and cook until al dente, about 8 minutes (typically
about 2 minutes less than the package instructions, unless they include
timing for al dente). Reserve about ¼ cup of the cooking water, then drain the
pasta well in a colander placed in the sink. Add the drained pasta to the pan
with the sauce and stir well to coat. Raise the heat to medium-high. Add the
shelled and shell-on mussels (and any liquid that accumulated in the bowl) to
the sauce and pasta and toss gently to coat. Add the reserved cooking water
as needed if the sauce seems dry. Fold in the parsley and serve right away.

PAN-SEARED SCALLOPS WITH AVOCADO AND SALSA

Perhaps the most delicate of the shellfish enjoyed from these waters, scallops have extremely tender flesh and a sweet, nutty flavor that shines with rich pairings and a bit of heat—making them perfect for this Latin American–inflected recipe. Be sure to buy "dry" scallops, not dehydrated scallops (which have been treated to soak up more moisture).

SERVES 6

36 dry sea scallops

2 ripe avocados, pitted and peeled

2 teaspoons mayonnaise

1 lime, halved

Kosher salt or sea salt and freshly ground black pepper

1 cup finely diced ripe plum tomatoes

2 scallions, white and tender green parts, finely chopped

1 teaspoon minced jalapeño chile (remove the seeds for less heat)

2 tablespoons chopped fresh cilantro

2 tablespoons canola oil or vegetable oil

1 Gently pat the scallops dry on paper towels. Set aside. In a small bowl, using a fork, mash the avocados with the mayonnaise until smooth. Add a squeeze of lime juice and a pinch each of salt and pepper. Taste and adjust the seasoning. Set aside.

2 In another small bowl, combine the tomatoes, scallions, jalapeño, and cilantro and stir gently to combine well. Season to taste with lime juice, salt, and pepper.

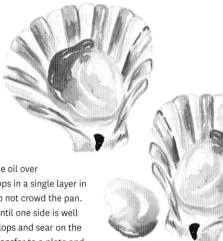

3 In a large, nonstick sauté pan, heat the oil over medium-high heat. Arrange the scallops in a single layer in the pan. Work in batches if necessary; do not crowd the pan. Sear the scallops without moving them until one side is well browned, about 2 minutes. Turn the scallops and sear on the second side in the same way. Carefully transfer to a plate and set aside to rest for about 2 minutes.

4 To serve, divide the avocado mixture among 6 plates, mounding it in the center of each. Arrange 6 scallops on top of the avocado on each plate. Spoon 1 teaspoon of the tomato salsa on top of each scallop. Serve right away.

DESSERTS &
BAKED GOODS

In the coastal Northeast, people wait all year for the brief but robust harvest of Cape Cod fruit. From strawberries to blueberries to apples, nothing tastes better than something you have longed for since the last bite savored last season.

These recipes from the sweet arena are straightforward and use fresh ingredients to elevate and shine a spotlight on local, seasonal fruit. Blueberries get a lift from fresh ginger in an updated classic pie and a lightening, brightening kick from lemons in a versatile pound cake. Most of these desserts would only get better with a scoop of ice cream from one of the many great shops from Bourne to Provincetown—or from your favorite local creamery.

APPLE CRISP

Apples can be found just about anywhere, but for many of us, a dessert baked with apples evokes fall in New England. As the days grow shorter, like Cape Codders, you'll appreciate how quick and easy this recipe is, and really value the payoff—the transporting aroma and taste of sweet, cooked apples laced with warming cinnamon spice and an irresistible sweet and crunchy topping.

SERVES 8

Unsalted butter for greasing, plus ½ cup (1 stick) cold unsalted butter, cut into ½-inch pieces

2 pounds of your favorite apples (4 or 5 medium to large apples)

2 tablespoons light brown sugar, plus ⅔ cup packed

1 tablespoon fresh lemon juice

½ cup all-purpose flour

½ cup old-fashioned rolled oats

¾ teaspoon ground cinnamon

Pinch of kosher salt or sea salt

1 Preheat the oven to 375°F. Butter a 2-quart baking dish. Peel the apples and cut in half lengthwise. Scoop out and discard the cores and seeds. Cut the apple halves lengthwise into slices ½ to ¾ inch thick and place in a large bowl. Sprinkle the 2 tablespoons brown sugar and the lemon juice over the top of the apples and toss gently until thoroughly coated. Transfer the apple slices to the prepared baking dish.

2 In a bowl, stir together the flour, the oats, the ⅔ cup brown sugar, the cinnamon, and the salt. Add the cold butter pieces and, using your fingers, rub the butter into the mixture until it is incorporated but still in very small lumps. Spread over the top of the apples.

3 Bake until the topping is browned and the apples are tender when pierced with a knife, 45 to 50 minutes. Transfer to a wire rack and let cool for about 10 minutes. Serve warm.

CRANBERRY GRANOLA

It doesn't matter how much you make—double, triple, or quadruple this recipe—it will still disappear in minutes. This granola is delicious and satisfying as is, but feel free to add your own favorite ingredients, such as dried ginger, sesame seeds, dried cherries, or raisins. Consider this a great housewarming or holiday gift; just pack into pretty glass jars and top with a festive bow.

MAKES ABOUT 6 CUPS; SERVES 4 TO 6

3 cups old-fashioned rolled oats

1 cup whole almonds

¾ cup unsweetened shredded coconut

⅓ cup packed light brown sugar

⅓ cup maple syrup

¼ cup vegetable oil

2 teaspoons ground cinnamon

¾ teaspoon kosher salt or sea salt

½ teaspoon ground allspice

1 cup chopped dried cranberries

1 Preheat the oven to 250°F. In a large bowl, combine the oats, almonds, coconut, and brown sugar.

2 In a small bowl, whisk together the maple syrup and oil. Add the wet ingredients to the dry ingredients and stir briefly. Add the cinnamon, salt, and allspice and stir to mix well.

3 Scrape half of the mixture onto each of 2 rimmed baking sheets and spread in a thin, even layer. Bake, stirring every 15 minutes, until evenly browned, about 1 hour and 15 minutes.

4 Transfer the pans to wire racks and let cool. When fully cooled, transfer the granola to a large bowl; add the cranberries and toss to mix well. Store in tightly sealed containers at room temperature for up to 2 weeks.

BLUEBERRY-GINGER PIE

Making a pie is the perfect way to celebrate the brief but beautiful blueberry season each summer—make as many as you have berries for. Once cooled completely, this pie freezes well. If fresh blueberries are unavailable, frozen blueberries will still make a great pie; do not thaw, but add 10 to 15 minutes to the baking time. This pie dough is great to have on hand in the freezer at all times: just double the recipe, roll the extra dough into a disk, wrap, label, and freeze for up to 4 months.

SERVES 8

1 recipe Pie Dough
(recipe follows)

4 cups fresh or frozen
blueberries

½ cup sugar, plus 1 teaspoon

2 tablespoons cornstarch

1 tablespoon fresh lemon juice

1 teaspoon lemon zest

1 tablespoon peeled and
grated fresh ginger

Pinch of kosher salt or sea salt

2 tablespoons cold unsalted
butter, cut into small pieces

1 large egg white

1 Make the pie dough as directed. Fold one rolled-out dough round in half and carefully transfer to a 9-inch pie dish. Unfold so that it fits over the entire dish. Shimmy the dough into the pie dish, without stretching it, and pat it firmly into the bottom and up the sides of the pan. Trim the edges of the dough, leaving a 1-inch overhang. Set aside until ready to use.

2 In a large bowl, combine the blueberries, the ½ cup sugar, the cornstarch, lemon juice and zest, ginger, and salt and stir gently until thoroughly combined. Spoon the blueberry mixture and any liquid in the bowl into the dough-lined pan. Scatter the top of the blueberries with the 2 tablespoons butter pieces. Lay the second dough round over the top of the blueberries, leaving about 1 inch of overhang. Fold the top edge of dough under the bottom edge of dough and trim the excess. Crimp the edges to seal. Make a few small incisions in the center of the top of the pie to allow steam to escape. Refrigerate the pie for 30 minutes.

3 Preheat the oven to 375°F. In a small bowl, whisk the egg white with 1 teaspoon water. Brush the top of the pie with the egg wash, then sprinkle the 1 teaspoon sugar over the top. Bake the pie until the pastry is a deep golden brown, the juices are bubbling, and the filling has thickened, 50 to 60 minutes. Transfer to a wire rack and let cool for at least 1 hour or completely. Cut into wedges and serve.

PIE DOUGH

MAKES DOUGH FOR 1 DOUBLE-CRUST PIE

2½ cups unbleached all-purpose flour, plus more for dusting

2 tablespoons sugar

¼ teaspoon kosher salt

1 cup (2 sticks) cold unsalted butter, cut into ¼-inch cubes

3 tablespoons ice water

In a food processor, pulse together the flour, sugar, and salt. Add the butter and pulse until the butter pieces are no larger than a pea. Add the ice water and pulse 3 or 4 times, or just until the dough begins to come together—it will be crumbly. Dump the shaggy dough onto a lightly floured work surface and squish the dough together without kneading or working the dough too much. Divide the dough into 2 same-sized balls, then flatten each into a disk about 1 inch thick. Cover with plastic wrap and refrigerate for at least 20 minutes and up to overnight.

When ready to use, on a lightly floured work surface, using a rolling pin, flatten one disk and roll top to bottom until a "tongue" shape is formed. Turn the so the dough piece is facing you horizontally and roll top to bottom until a 12-inch circle is formed. Dust the work surface, the rolling pin, and your hands with flour as needed to prevent sticking. Repeat with second disk.

BLUEBERRY-LEMON POUND CAKE

Blueberries and lemons are natural companions in the kitchen and on the palate, and complement each other extremely pleasingly in baked goods. The addition of yogurt to this recipe keeps things rich, as a pound cake ought to be, but manages to lighten and brighten at the same time. This is a cake recipe, but certainly does well as a muffin, too; see instructions and altered cooking times in the method.

SERVES 8

Unsalted butter for greasing, plus ½ cup, at room temperature

4 tablespoons all-purpose flour, plus 3 cups

2 cups sugar

4 ounces cream cheese

Zest of 1 lemon

3 large eggs plus 1 large egg white

2 cups fresh or frozen blueberries

1 teaspoon vanilla extract

1 teaspoon baking powder

½ teaspoon baking soda

½ teaspoon salt

1 cup lemon-flavored yogurt

1 Preheat the oven to 350°F. Butter a 10-inch tube pan or Bundt pan or a standard 12-cup muffin tin. Add 2 tablespoons of the flour and shake to coat all the sides of the pan. Knock out and discard any excess flour. Set aside.

2 In the bowl of a stand mixer fitted with the whisk attachment or using a hand mixer in a large bowl, combine the sugar, the ½ cup butter, the cream cheese, and the lemon zest. Beat in the eggs and egg white, one at a time, making sure each egg is fully incorporated before adding another. Set aside.

3 In a medium bowl, combine 2 tablespoons flour with the blueberries and stir gently until thoroughly coated (this will help prevent the berries from sinking to the bottom of the pan during baking). Set aside.

4 In a large bowl, whisk together the 3 cups flour, the vanilla, the baking powder, baking soda, and salt. With the mixer on low, add about one-fourth of the flour mixture and about one-third of the yogurt to the batter and beat to incorporate. Repeat, alternating the flour and yogurt and ending with flour, until everything is incorporated—be careful not to overmix. Carefully fold in the blueberries.

5 Pour the batter into the prepared cake pan or muffin tin and bake until the tops are no longer wet and a toothpick inserted into the middle of the cake or a muffin comes out with dry crumbs, about 1 hour and 10 minutes for the cake pans or 30 to 35 minutes for the muffins. Transfer to a wire rack and let cool for about 10 minutes in the pan. Remove the cake or muffins from the pan and let cool completely on the rack. If you made a cake, cut into wedges. Serve right away.

STRAWBERRY-RHUBARB CRUMBLE

With its elephant-ear leaves and gem-red stalks, rhubarb is a welcome and often whimsical sight, and grows easily and prolifically in many Cape Cod gardens. It can be too tart on its own, but famously paired with its best friend, the strawberry, rhubarb gets tamed enough to shine. In this crumble, a double dose of almond and lots of cinnamon takes it over the top.

▊▊▊▊▊ **SERVES 8**

2 pounds rhubarb stalks (about 10), ends trimmed and stringy bits removed, cut crosswise into slices about ½ inch thick

1 cup packed dark brown sugar

1 pound strawberries, hulled and cut into slices about ½ inch thick

2 tablespoons cornstarch

1 teaspoon fresh lemon juice

1 teaspoon almond extract

½ cup (1 stick) unsalted butter, at room temperature

1½ cups packed light brown sugar

1½ cups all-purpose flour

1¼ cups old-fashioned rolled oats

¾ cup slivered almonds

1½ teaspoons ground cinnamon

¾ teaspoon kosher salt

1 Preheat the oven to 375°F. In a medium bowl, combine the rhubarb with ½ cup of the dark brown sugar; set aside.

2 In a large bowl, combine the strawberries with the remaining ½ cup dark brown sugar; set aside.

3 After about 10 minutes, drain and discard any rhubarb juice that accumulated in the bowl and add the rhubarb to the strawberries. Add the cornstarch, lemon juice, and almond extract to the fruit and stir gently until thoroughly mixed. Transfer the fruit mixture to a 9-by-13-inch baking dish and spread in an even layer.

4 In another bowl, combine the butter, light brown sugar, flour, oats, almonds, cinnamon, and salt and toss, using your fingers or a pastry cutter, until large (2-inch) clumps of dough form. Evenly distribute the clumps of dough on top of the fruit mixture. Bake until the topping is golden brown and the juices are bubbling, about 45 minutes. Let rest for 15 minutes, then cut into squares and serve.

PORTUGUESE SWEET BREAD

More kudos to the kitchens of Provincetown or "P Town," where this traditional sweet bread can be found in most home kitchens and every bakery. Lightly toasted and slathered with butter and summer berry jam, this bread is morning nirvana. To turbo-boost your day, try this as the base for French toast or bread pudding.

MAKES 2 ROUND 9-INCH LOAVES

Unsalted butter for greasing

All-purpose flour for dusting, plus 5½ cups

2 tablespoons active dry yeast

¼ cup warm (100°F) water

1 cup warm (100°F) milk

¾ cup sugar, plus 1 teaspoon

½ cup (1 stick) unsalted butter, at room temperature

3 large eggs, plus 1 egg white

1 teaspoon kosher salt or sea salt

Vegetable oil for greasing

1 Butter the bottom and sides of two 9-inch cake pans. Sprinkle in flour and tip to coat on all sides. Tap out and discard any excess flour. Set the pans aside.

2 In a large bowl, dissolve the yeast in the warm water. Stir in the warm milk, the ¾ cup sugar, the butter, whole eggs, and salt. Add the 5½ cups flour and stir until a rough dough forms. Turn out the dough onto a lightly floured work surface and knead until smooth and elastic, about 5 minutes. Place the dough in a lightly oiled bowl, cover, and let rise until doubled in size, 1 to 1½ hours.

3 Punch down the dough, gently knead 2 or 3 times, and divide in half. Shape each half into a ball and gently tuck the outer edges of the dough ball underneath to create some tension on the top. Place each loaf in a prepared pan. Cover each with a clean kitchen towel and let rise until doubled in size, about 1 hour.

4 Preheat the oven to 350°F. In a small bowl, whisk the egg white with 1 teaspoon water. Brush the top of each loaf with the egg wash, then sprinkle with the 1 teaspoon sugar. Bake until golden brown, about 40 minutes. Let cool on a wire rack, about 20 minutes, then slice and serve.

INDEX